GLOBAL CITIZENSHIP

Valuing World Heritage

A⁺

SUSAN WATSON

This edition first published in 2004 in the United States of America by Smart Apple Media.

Smart Apple Media
1980 Lookout Drive
North Mankato
Minnesota 56003

Library of Congress Cataloging-in-Publication Data

Watson, Susan, 1949–
    Valuing world heritage / Susan Watson.
    p.cm. — (Global citizenship)

    Summary: Describes ways in which appreciation of and protection of our diverse cultural heritages help make us all citizens of the whole world.

    ISBN 1-58340-401-5
    1. World Heritage areas. 2. Cultural property. 3. World citizenship. 4. Globalization. [1. Globalization. 2. Historic sites.] I. Title.
    G140.5.W38 2003
    909—dc21   2002044615

First Edition
9 8 7 6 5 4 3 2 1

First published in 2003 by
MACMILLAN EDUCATION AUSTRALIA PTY LTD
627 Chapel Street, South Yarra, Australia 3141

Associated companies and representatives throughout the world.

Packaged for Macmillan Education Australia by Publishing Options Pty Ltd
Text design by Gail McManus Graphics
Cover design by Dimitrios Frangoulis
Illustrations by Infographics Pty Ltd
Page make-up by Crackerjack Desktop Services

Printed in Thailand

Acknowledgements

The author is especially grateful to Matthew, Kyja, CJ, and Samantha for being the model global citizens of this series. The author and the publisher are grateful to the following for permission to reproduce copyright materials:

Cover photograph: Great Barrier Reef, courtesy of Mark A. Johnson © 2002.

Jean-Paul Ferrero/Auscape International, p. 19 (top); Ferrero–Labat/Auscape International, p. 15 (center); Tui De Roy/Auscape International, p. 28 (right); Colin Monteath/Auscape International, p. 21 (top right); Australian Picture Library/Corbis, pp. 9 (top right), 12–13 (center), 18 (top); Coo-ee Picture Library, pp. 7, 14 (top), 15 (bottom), 25 (top); Getty Images, pp. 10 (right), 11 (left), 15 (top), 20, 21 (left), 22 (top), 24 (bottom), 27 (top right), 29 (bottom); The G.R. "Dick" Roberts Photo Library, p. 17 (bottom); Imageaddict, p. 23 (right); © 2002 Mark A. Johnson, p. 26 (bottom); Legend Images, p. 8; National Archives of Australia, p. 13 (top); Neil McLeod, p. 17 (top); Pelusey Photography, p. 14 (center); Pioneer Settlement Museum Swan Hill, Victoria, pp. 4–5 (center); Reuters, p. 6; Sarah Saunders, p. 9 (top left); David Hancock/Skyscans, p. 19 (bottom); Susan Watson, pp. 4 (far left), 4 (center left), 4 (center right), 4 (far right), 10 (left), 11 (right), 12 (left), 16 (top), 30.

While every care has been taken to trace and acknowledge copyright, the publisher tenders their apologies for any accidental infringement where copyright has proved untraceable. Where the attempt has been unsuccessful, the publisher welcomes information that would redress the situation.

Please note

At the time of printing, the Internet addresses appearing in this book were correct. Owing to the dynamic nature of the Internet, however, we cannot guarantee that all these addresses will remain correct.

Contents

Global citizens

A global citizen is a person who:
◎ has rights and responsibilities
◎ acts in a caring way based on knowledge and understanding
◎ relates to others within their family, friendship groups, community, and country
◎ develops personal values and commitments
◎ develops a sense of their own role in the world.

A study of global citizenship will help you understand how people affect the quality of global environments and the well-being of others. Active global citizens do not just sit back and wait for others to do something. They turn their ideas into action. Action can take many forms:
◎ volunteering by giving time, help, and ideas freely
◎ talking to your friends
◎ thinking deeply
◎ learning more
◎ taking part in community events.

Throughout this book Allira, Harry, Lin, and Denzel will tell you their ways of acting as global citizens. We can all care for each other and our environment.

citizen
a person who lives in a large group of people who they mix with

environments
natural and built surroundings

ALLIRA

Hi! I'm Allira. I live in a country town near the sea. My family background is Aboriginal–Australian.

we are global citizens

HARRY

Hello. I'm Harry. I live with my family in a suburb of a big modern city of four million people.

Global citizens value world heritage

Active global citizens know something about the past of their:

◎ family
◎ local neighborhood
◎ state
◎ country
◎ world.

They use this understanding to help them value things that have survived from the past. These things can be in nature or part of different cultures. They make up the world's heritage.

Global citizens know who they are and about their cultural backgrounds. Valuing the world's heritage helps global citizens make decisions about the present. They can help make sure that the world's heritage is left for others to share in the future.

cultures
groups of people with different customs, values, and beliefs

heritage
things from the past and present that are valued and saved for future generations

Global citizens can learn about their country's heritage by visiting historical theme parks.

We are global citizens

LIN

I'm Lin. I migrated to my new country with my parents. We live with my grandparents who came 15 years ago from Malaysia.

DENZEL

Hi! I'm Denzel. My mom and I live in a high-rise apartment close to the city center. We're African-American.

5

Our past is our history

history
the study of past events

archaeologists
scientists who dig up the remains from people's past lives and study them

indigenous people
groups with the same language and culture who are related to the first people in an area

It is important for all global citizens to know something about the world's past. This is called history. There are different ways of learning about the history of a place, building, or event:

◎ looking at old buildings and monuments
◎ reading books about the past
◎ studying old documents and maps
◎ learning from archaeologists who dig up old remains
◎ listening to older people talking about their lives when they were young
◎ hearing stories or singing songs about days gone by
◎ visiting museums and galleries
◎ walking in national parks
◎ watching historical films or television documentaries.

Digging up the remains of places where people used to live is the way that archaeology connects us to our past history.

 CASE STUDY **What Lake Mungo's past tells us**

The Lake Mungo region of far western New South Wales in Australia is of special historical significance.

Archaeologists, working with the local indigenous people, have dug up the remains of Australia's original inhabitants and have dated these back to at least 60,000 years ago. A skeleton from the area was covered in red ocher. This means that the earthy mixture was probably used for religious or artistic reasons. This would probably be the world's earliest use of paint.

As archaeologists keep digging in the Lake Mungo region, they continue to discover more and more about the past lives of Aboriginal-Australians. They are careful to dig in an orderly way so that they do not destroy any of the remains.

The Seven Wonders of the Ancient World

For more than 5,000 years, people have been building structures that are almost beyond belief in their size and beauty. The main reasons for building such structures are:

◎ as religious shrines
◎ as burial places
◎ for defense
◎ for artistic beauty
◎ for scientific research
◎ as a display of power and wealth.

Many of the buildings of the ancient world survived hundreds, and sometimes thousands, of years. They were valued so much that during the Middle Ages (A.D. 1450–1600), a list was made. It was called "The Seven Wonders of the Ancient World."

The Seven Wonders of the Ancient World were concentrated in a small region close to the Mediterranean Sea that is today bordered by Greece, Turkey, Syria, and Egypt. It is near the two large rivers in the Middle East, the Tigris and the Euphrates.

GLOBAL FACT

The oldest of The Seven Wonders of the Ancient World is the Great Pyramid at Giza in Egypt. Remarkably, it is the only one that survives even today.

shrines
holy places
mausoleum
a huge burial tomb

The Seven Wonders of the Ancient World

Great Pyramid of Cheops at Giza built around 2,500 B.C.

Temple of Artemis at Ephesus built around 550 B.C.

Hanging Gardens of Babylon built around 500 B.C.

Statue of Zeus at Olympia built around 450 B.C.

Mausoleum of Halicarnassus built around 350 B.C.

Lighthouse of Alexandria built around 290 B.C.

Colossus of Rhodes built around 270 B.C.

The Hanging Gardens of Babylon on the east bank of the Euphrates River in Iraq was one of The Seven Wonders of the Ancient World.

From generation to generation

generation
people of about the same age group and living at the same time

preserve
to keep something safe so that it will last for a long time

Most people have one thing in common. It is something from our past that we have kept and valued. This might be a special toy, a diary, a photo album, a collection of stamps or trading cards, or an old car. When something is passed down through a family over a long period of time, it has been passed down from one generation to the next. In a family with grandparents, parents, and children all living, there are three generations of the same family.

Family heirlooms connect us to the past

Many families have heirlooms that they value and want to keep in the same family over time. Items such as jewelry, furniture, sacred books, paintings, and musical instruments are examples of heirlooms. Heirlooms can vary with people's backgrounds:

◎ a Christian family could have an old Bible
◎ a Pacific Islander family might have a specially carved wooden statue decorated with mother-of-pearl
◎ a Japanese family might keep a beautiful silk kimono.

Photo albums and diaries connect us to the past

A common way of keeping a record of our past is through photos, usually kept in an album. The album helps preserve the photos so they will not get damaged.

Diaries also tell something about the past. A diary is usually a private account of the everyday life of a person. If diaries are preserved, they can be used to tell something about the past to younger generations.

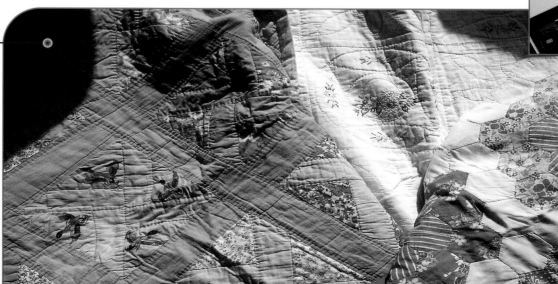

Family heirlooms, such as this beautiful handsewn quilt, are a way of families connecting to their past.

Storytelling connects us to the past

Books and reading material became available to large numbers of people in European society in the 1800s. Until then, storytelling was the main way of passing down history from one generation to the next. Storytelling is a form of oral history because it is spoken and not written. It is still common to people who do not have daily access to books, radio, and TV.

Older people connect us to the past

Grandparents are usually 40 to 80 years older than their grandchildren. They have had a lot of life experiences and seen a lot of change since they were young children. People of the older generation are a valuable way of learning about the past.

In Japan, some older people who are experts in traditional skills are valued as living national treasures. Such people pass down their skills and knowledge to younger Japanese people so that these are preserved.

national treasures
people or things of very special importance to a whole country's history and pride

This puppet-maker is a living national treasure in Japan. It is important for his traditional skills to be passed on to future generations.

Old photos in an album help preserve the past.

What can I do?
I'm really lucky because my great grandfather is still alive. He's 93 and grew up in China in the early 1900s. He's seen lots of change and lived in two different countries. I can learn so much from him.

Cultural practices

All people have a set of beliefs, customs, and values within their society or group. This is their culture. The word "culture" can be used to describe different groups or ways of living, such as:

◎ Australian-Aboriginal culture
◎ North American culture
◎ Jewish culture
◎ youth culture
◎ westernized culture
◎ Ancient Greek culture
◎ Pacific Island culture
◎ pop culture.

Religion is one of the main parts of culture for many people. Religious beliefs have usually been passed down through hundreds, and even thousands, of years. People follow traditions as part of their culture and religion. Traditions set a culture apart from other groups. Some are passed down through the generations, such as:

◎ In some Christian countries, there is a Christmas tradition of decorating a small pine tree, putting presents under it, and having a roast dinner with the family.

◎ An Islamic tradition is for a richer family to kill a goat or a sheep at a special time each year. It is roasted on a spit. Seven poorer families from the neighborhood are invited to eat it.

Cultural heritage includes such traditions. It also includes things built by people as part of their culture. Cultural heritage is part of everyone's heritage.

traditions
the parts of a culture that are passed down from generation to generation

This cathedral is typical of European cultural heritage in which Christianity is the main form of religion.

Beautiful mosques are part of the cultural heritage of the Islamic religion.

The natural environment

Natural heritage comes from the natural environment around us. When places and things in nature survive over many generations, they become part of the world's natural heritage. We experience natural heritage when we look at things, such as a:

◎ beautiful forest landscape
◎ plant, animal, or insect living in its habitat
◎ volcano
◎ rocky shoreline
◎ habitat supporting a wide range of life.

We can also feel and hear parts of our natural heritage, such as:

◎ fresh, clean air on a mountain top
◎ ocean waves rolling onto the shore
◎ many different bird and animal sounds on an African grassland plain.

habitat
the place where a plant, animal, or insect lives and reproduces

The elephant's habitat on the African grasslands is a part of the world's natural heritage.

This beautiful tree-fern gully is also part of our natural heritage.

What can I do?
I know of a special rockpool area at the beach we go to for vacation. I'm going to look at it much more closely next time. There's lots of different sea creatures and plants. I'll make a poster about them to show my class.

Preserving cultural heritage

archives
places where public records and historical documents are kept

In the same way as people keep and protect something special, the wider community also preserves its heritage. A community's cultural heritage can be preserved in many places:

◎ museums
◎ old buildings
◎ historical theme parks
◎ local historical societies

◎ galleries
◎ archives
◎ oral history on tape in libraries
◎ statues and monuments.

Museums

Since ancient times, people have wanted to preserve objects for future generations. Special buildings called museums are used to store these objects. Museums allow the objects to be displayed so that the general public can view their heritage. Museums also do the work of fixing the objects if they become damaged or worn from age.

GLOBAL FACT

One of the world's first museums was built in Alexandria, Egypt, more than 2,300 years ago.

Museums help preserve a community's cultural heritage through protecting and displaying objects from the past.

Art galleries

restoring
repairing something to bring it back to a good condition

Another type of place where objects are displayed is an art gallery. Art galleries contain works of art such as paintings, drawings, sculptures, photos, glassware, and ceramic pots. Some workers in art galleries have the job of restoring old or damaged works of art to help preserve them.

Archives

Historical documents and other materials such as photos and films are preserved in places called archives. Large libraries also contain archives of old books. Oral history is also stored in this way, usually on audiotape. Archives are important to historians because they are a source of original documents.

Historians use original documents to study details about the past.

Old buildings

Cultural heritage can be seen in the buildings and other structures, such as bridges and monuments, that survive through the ages. Many of these were built of stone. Stone wears away over time due to rain, wind, and other weather conditions. Pollution from car fumes and damage by people also harm them. Efforts need to be made to preserve and repair old buildings as part of our cultural heritage.

Restoring old works of art helps preserve them for the future.

What can I do?
Historical theme parks are another way of preserving our past. Our class is going to visit one soon. We'll learn what it was like to live in days gone by.

Preserving natural heritage

Natural heritage is made up of things in the natural environment that are preserved for future generations. When something is preserved in nature, this is called conservation. Most countries in the world have a system of national parks in which nature conservation is practiced. In national parks, all of the plants, animals, and insects are protected as well as the rocks, soil, and water.

conservation
keeping areas of the natural environment in their original condition

Park rangers work in national parks to help supervise and run them. The rangers make sure that visitors to the park do not harm the natural environment. They also run education sessions to help visitors better understand their natural environment and the importance of its heritage.

Signs in national parks make people aware that they have to protect the plants and animals in them.

Park rangers have special knowledge about the plants and animals in their national park. They share this with visitors to help them value natural heritage.

What can I do?
There are two national parks close to home. I'm going to visit them with my family to find out all their special features. I'll try to talk to a park ranger and ask about what they do too!

National parks around the world

There are many national parks throughout the world. Each has its own unique natural heritage that should be valued and preserved.

CASE STUDY **Three outstanding national parks**

Yellowstone National Park, U.S.

Yellowstone National Park is in the southwest corner of the state of Wyoming. It became the world's first national park when it was established in 1872. The government wanted to conserve the many wonders of the Yellowstone River area for the enjoyment of the people. The most outstanding feature of the national park is its number of active geysers. Geysers are springs that break through Earth's surface as hot water and steam. Yellowstone has more geysers than the total in the rest of the world.

Kruger National Park, South Africa

Kruger National Park is in the northeast corner of South Africa. It is nearly 5 million acres (2,000,000 h) in area. The park was established in 1898 to protect some of the famous African wildlife. Kruger National Park is best known for the "big five" in African wildlife—the lion, elephant, leopard, buffalo, and rhinoceros. There are more than 1,800 protected lions in the park. Visitors can travel in their cars through the park to view the animals in the wild.

Kosciuszko National Park, Australia

Kosciuszko National Park is in the southeast corner of the state of New South Wales. It covers 2,700 square miles (nearly 7,000 sq km) of the Snowy Mountains and features Mount Kosciuszko, which is Australia's highest mountain at 7,310 feet (2,228 m). The park is important in conserving some of Australia's unique alpine plants and animals, which are found in high mountain areas.

Indigenous heritage

A special part of the world's heritage comes from indigenous groups. There are about 350 million indigenous people in more than 70 countries around the globe. They are descendants of the original people in an area. Evidence of the way their ancestors lived can be found in things like ancient tools, rock paintings and carvings, wooden bowls, kitchen scraps, and house materials.

Many indigenous groups still speak their own languages and have their own cultural practices.

Scarred trees like this are part of indigenous heritage. The scar shows where bark was scraped out to make a canoe or to be used for shelter.

Indigenous groups	Location
Australian-Aboriginal and Torres Strait Islander peoples	Throughout Australia. Each group has its own connection to particular areas.
Sami (previously known as Lapps)	Northern part of Scandinavia in the Arctic and subarctic areas of Norway, Sweden, Finland, and western Russia
Inuit (previously known as Eskimo)	Arctic area of northern Canada, particularly the new Canadian territory of Nunavut
Hopi (Native Americans)	Southwest area of the U.S., especially around Arizona
Karen	Northern Thai-Burma border
Kurds	Eastern Turkey, northern Syria, and Iraq
Tamil	Northern Sri Lanka and southern India
Masai	Kenya and Tanzania in East Africa

What can I do?

There's a scarred tree on a riverbank in my town. It's an important part of my Aboriginal–Australian heritage. My community has told its story and written this on a sign in front of the tree. We want others to respect the tree too.

Indigenous groups at a glance

There are groups of indigenous people in Australia and the United States. Aboriginal and Torres Strait Islander peoples and the Native American Hopi are some of them.

urban cities and towns

GLOBAL FACT
The International Decade of the World's Indigenous People was from 1994–2003. It recognized the importance of indigenous heritage.

Aboriginal and Torres Strait Islander peoples

CASE STUDY

Over many thousands of years, indigenous peoples have left signs of their occupation of Australia. The reminders of where people lived, where they ate or collected food, how they hunted, their art, and their sacred sites are all a special part of Australia's heritage. Aboriginal rock painting is one of the world's oldest forms of art.

At the time of the first European settlers in 1788, there were estimated to be more than 350,000 Aboriginal people. They were hunter-gatherers who lived in small family groups. Aboriginal and Torres Strait Islander peoples believe they have always lived in Australia and belong to the land and the sea. They use Dreaming stories to explain the environment and their traditional law.

Today, many live and work in towns and cities. Urban groups still value their cultural background.

Hopi of southwest U.S.

CASE STUDY

Hopi people belong to one of the many Native American tribes that have survived hundreds of years of change. From 1540 onwards, Spanish soldiers, then European settlers invaded their lands in the southwest corner of the North American continent. Hopi people live in the oldest continuously occupied villages in the entire country.

The lives of Hopi people today are very different from those of their ancestors. Yet they still value the traditions and beliefs of their past. The principles of harmony and balance are guiding ideals. Farming remains an important activity for many Hopi people. The traditional crops of corn, beans, and squash are still planted and highly prized.

Indigenous rights

Most indigenous peoples have strong spiritual links to the land and the sea. This has shaped their beliefs and culture. Another common link is that indigenous peoples want to pass down their heritage to future generations. Global citizens need to value the cultures of indigenous peoples to help them survive into the future.

Land rights and self-government

Indigenous heritage is not just the traditions and beliefs, art, and religion of the culture. Land, and the sea close to the land, are part of the original heritage of indigenous peoples. Land rights will help them get some of their land back. The right to run their own affairs is also something indigenous peoples want. This is self-government.

Many indigenous groups, such as New Zealand's Maori, want to be given back some of the land of their ancestors.

 CASE STUDY Land rights in Canada

There is a system of land rights in Canada. This is because indigenous groups such as the Inuit have occupied and used the land over a long time. They have been given the right to hunt, trap, and fish on the land occupied by their ancestors. Inuit people were also given the right to self-government in a new territory. On April 1, 1999, one of Canada's existing territories was divided in two. This created a new territory called Nunavut, which means "our land" in the language of Inuit people. Nunavut is an area one-fifth the size of all of Canada. Inuit people make up 80 percent of the population of Nunavut. They have an equal say along with the Canadian government in the running of their territory.

Land rights in conflict

It is not always easy for everyone to agree about the heritage of indigenous peoples. There are often disagreements about how the land should be used, especially if it is rich in minerals that can be mined and sold for a lot of money.

uranium
a radioactive metal that is used to produce nuclear energy and weapons

 CASE STUDY **The fight for traditional lands in Kakadu**

Kakadu National Park covers an area of 7,722 square miles (20,000 sq km) in the north part of Australia's Northern Territory. It is a very special area of wetlands and Australia's largest national park. Its cultural heritage contains many important Aboriginal rock art sites. Its natural heritage includes a wide range of plant, animal, and insect life. The area also contains rich deposits of uranium. There is already one uranium mine in the park. This is the Ranger Uranium Mine.

More than one-third of Kakadu National Park now belongs to Aboriginal groups. One of these groups is the Mirrar who want to protect their land from further mining. During the late 1990s, two women from the Mirrar group organized public protests. Jacqui Katona and Yvonne Margarula did not want a second mine at Jabiluka to be built on their traditional land. They said: "Jabiluka is about protecting culture for future generations and continuing to live the cultural traditions."

Many ordinary citizens also did not agree with the mine and they supported the Mirrar people. In March 2001, the mining company, which has a lease on the Jabiluka site, decided not to build the mine for at least 10 years. This was because of the disagreement from the traditional owners and citizens of the wider community.

World Heritage sites

Many places in the world have outstanding value. A special international committee was formed in 1972 to help protect them. This is the World Heritage Committee. It has 21 members from different world countries and is part of the United Nations Educational Scientific and Cultural Organization (UNESCO).

Countries put forward places they think have world heritage value. The World Heritage Committee makes decisions about these places. The committee publishes a list of the places that they think have outstanding value to the whole world. The list is called the World Heritage List. When it started in 1972 there were 12 sites. At the beginning of 2002, there were 730 sites on the list.

When a place is put on the World Heritage List it becomes a World Heritage site. Sites are either cultural or natural. Many sites are spectacular in their beauty, such as Mount Kenya National Park in eastern Africa, Australia's Great Barrier Reef, or the U.S.'s Grand Canyon of Arizona. There are other less beautiful sites that are also worth saving, not for how they look, but for what they mean. The Auschwitz Concentration Camp in Poland is an example of this type of site on the list. Historians believe that 1.5 million people were starved, tortured, and murdered in this camp between 1940 and 1945. This was during World War II when Adolf Hitler ruled Germany.

The Auschwitz–Birkenau camp is on the World Heritage List as a symbol of the cruelty of some people to fellow human beings. Many of the people who were sent there were Jews.

Cultural World Heritage sites

A cultural heritage site on the World Heritage List must be at least one of the following:

◎ an example of people's creative brilliance
◎ an important development in new architecture or design
◎ an example of a cultural tradition that has disappeared or is related to an existing culture
◎ an outstanding example of human settlement or land use.

Natural World Heritage sites

A natural heritage site on the World Heritage List must be at least one of the following:

◎ an example of a stage in Earth's history
◎ a significant community of plants and animals living together, especially if they are threatened
◎ an area of exceptional beauty.

The Los Glaciares National Park at the southern tip of Argentina in South America is a natural World Heritage site. It is an area of exceptional natural beauty, with rugged, towering mountains, and glacial lakes.

The Parthenon on the Acropolis in Athens, Greece, is a cultural World Heritage site. It has universal value for its architecture. It was built nearly 2,500 years ago.

What can I do?

One of the best ways to get involved with World Heritage is to visit a World Heritage site if there is one near you. If you can't go in person, use the Internet to take a virtual tour. Learn as much as possible about the site and why it's part of our world's heritage.

Four cultural World Heritage sites

pharaoh
a ruler of ancient
Egypt

Four of the world's cultural World Heritage sites are the Pyramid, the Great Wall of China, the Taj Mahal, and the Statue of Liberty.

CASE STUDY **The Pyramid Fields at Giza, Egypt**

The capital of Ancient Egypt was Memphis. It stood near the center of today's capital, Cairo. On the edge of the city the Egyptians built a huge cemetery field. This field at Giza contains some amazing monuments including rock tombs, ornate temples, and gigantic pyramids, which became the burial places of the rulers of the country. One of the pyramids—the Great Pyramid—is one of the Seven Wonders of the Ancient World. It was built more than 4,500 years ago and still stands today.

Today, the Great Pyramid is enclosed with the other pyramids and the Sphinx in a tourist region. Also in the area is the museum housing the mysterious Sun Boat, which was only discovered in 1954. Archaeologists believe that the boat was used to carry the body of the pharaoh Khufu in his last journey on Earth before being buried inside the pyramid.

The Great Pyramid is still among the world's largest structures, standing almost as tall as a 50-story skyscraper. This is the largest of the Giza pyramids. It has enough room at its base to fit more than seven football fields. When the Great Pyramid was new, it had 2,300,000 stone blocks averaging more than 2.7 tons (2.5 t) each in weight. The biggest blocks weighed more than 16.5 tons (15 t). Except for passageways and chambers, the pyramid is solid. Every block of stone had to be dug from the earth, shaped, brought to the site, and lifted into place by people without modern machines.

One of the main issues facing this site is the huge number of tourists that visit. People tramping around the tombs are gradually wearing the stone away. Another problem is the graffiti that has been scrawled on some of the walls.

The site was added to the World Heritage List in 1979.

Astronauts can see the entire length of China's Great Wall from their spaceships.

CASE STUDY

The Great Wall, China

The world's greatest wall is a giant **military** structure. It has historic and architectural significance. It took shape around 2,200 years ago. Individual defense walls had been built in different states of China. These were joined to form what we now call the Great Wall.

At that time, First Emperor of Qin had to protect the entire Chinese empire from invasion from the north. He ordered the building of a giant wall that would link the smaller ones. The Great Wall stretched 4,163 miles (6,700 km) across the country's hilltops. This gave it high points for the 25,000 watchtowers that were built along it. Military guards used a system of flags and fires to signal each other from one tower to the other.

The Great Wall was renovated from time to time after the Qin Dynasty. A major renovation started with the founding of the Ming Dynasty in 1368, and took 200 years to complete. Today's wall is mostly the result of this effort. It was added to the World Heritage List in 1987.

People have caused damage to the wall. Local people have taken pieces of it to use for building material for farms and villages. The number of tourists is another problem as they can cause the stone to wear down. Restoration work is very slow and costs a lot.

military
to do with the army

RUSSIA

Great Wall

Yellow Sea

C H I N A

CASE STUDY: Taj Mahal, India

There is a huge mausoleum of white marble, built in Agra, India, between 1631 and 1648. It was ordered by Emperor Shah Jahan in memory of his favorite wife. It is called the Taj Mahal. The Taj is considered one of the most spectacular buildings of the world and is a beautiful example of Muslim architecture. It was added to the World Heritage List in 1983.

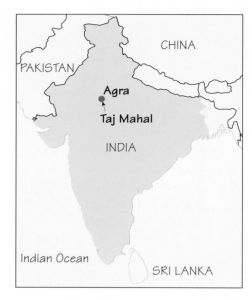

There are 26 guardians who help protect the Taj from the harm of vandals and too many tourists. Tourists come to visit from all over the world. They must take their shoes off before going inside. However, some tourists do not read the instructions and leave them on. It is a sign of respect in the Muslim faith to leave shoes at the front door.

The Taj Mahal is under threat. People, sandstorms, and pollution are battering it. The Taj may have to be closed to preserve it. It is suffering from 10 million tourists each year, and parts of the mausoleum are cracked and worn from overuse. There is also pollution from vehicles, brick-making factories, and iron foundries in Agra, one of the most polluted cities in India. The area immediately around the Taj has improved substantially since a Supreme Court ruling in 1999 that forced 260 iron foundries to change from wood and coal fuel to gas. However, by then, much of the damage had been done.

Statue of Liberty, U.S.

Next to the national flag, the Statue of Liberty is the most famous symbol of freedom for the United States. It is also a symbol of freedom for people from other countries, and was added to the World Heritage List in 1984.

> **carat**
> a measurement of the amount of pure gold in metal

The statue is sometimes called Lady Liberty. It was a gift from the French to remember the American Revolution, which led to independence in 1776. It is a gigantic sculpture built by famous sculptor Frederic-Auguste Bartholdi. He worked on it in Paris, then it was shipped from France to New York. The statue stands on Bedloe's Island, now known as Liberty Island. Ships traveling to the city of New York pass in front of the statue.

In 1986 the statue needed a large restoration job. This cost nearly $70 million. A new gold torch was added to replace the original one, which had been eaten away by salt. The torch is coated with 24-carat pure gold paint.

These are some interesting facts about the Statue of Liberty:

- It is 305 feet (93 m) high and 354 steps lead from the entrance to the crown.
- The seven rays of Lady Liberty's crown represent the seven seas and seven continents.
- The base on which the statue stands is set within the walls of an army fort. It was the largest concrete mass ever poured.
- There are 25 windows in Lady Liberty's crown. These symbolize the 25 gemstones found on Earth.
- The tablet, which the statue holds in her left hand, reads (in Roman numerals) "July 4th, 1776." This is the day the U.S. declared independence (freedom) from Britain.

mollusk
a soft-bodied sea creature, often having a shell

runoff
the rainwater that runs over the land and into rivers, lakes, and seas

Four natural World Heritage sites

Four of the world's Natural Heritage sites are the Great Barrier Reef, South Westland, the Galapagos Islands, and the Giant's Causeway.

GLOBAL FACT

It is illegal to remove coral from the Great Barrier Reef.

CASE STUDY ## Great Barrier Reef, Australia

The Great Barrier Reef is the world's largest coral reef. It stretches from the sea off the northern tip of Queensland to about 740 miles (2,300 km) south. The total area of the reef is five times the size of the Australian state of Tasmania.

In 1981, the Great Barrier Reef was added to the World Heritage List because it is a site of remarkable variety and beauty. It contains the world's largest collection of coral reefs. There are 400 types of coral, 1,500 species of fish, and 4,000 types of mollusk. The reef is also important for scientific study. It is the habitat of species such as the dugong (sea cow) and the large green turtle, which are threatened with extinction.

Tourism is the main industry in the Great Barrier Reef World Heritage Area. The numbers of tourists are increasing every year. Most tourists go to a very small area of the reef near the northern Queensland coast. This has caused damage in this area.

Another threat to the reef is the pollution that comes from rivers being washed into the sea, especially during heavy rainstorms. More and more people want to live close to the coast. Housing and farming pollute the runoff with chemicals and waste. This is harming the coral and other sea life.

CASE STUDY

South Westland, New Zealand

A large area in the southwest part of New Zealand's South Island was added to the World Heritage List in 1991. The area contains the Fiordland National Park with its 14 fiords. The landscape has been shaped by different periods of glaciation into:

- fiords
- rocky coasts
- towering cliffs
- glacial lakes
- waterfalls.

Much of the area is covered with beautiful beech trees, some of which are over 800 years old. The kea is the only alpine parrot in the world. It lives in the park, as does the rare and endangered takahe, a large flightless bird.

One of the most famous features of the park is Milford Sound, with Mitre Peak and its spectacular waterfalls, which tumble down almost vertical cliffs.

The national park has only a few roads. Not many people live there. It is one of the most popular walking-track areas of the world. The Milford Track is known as the "sightseeing and walking capital of the world." It is important that walkers and other tourists to the area respect the natural beauty and not harm the environment.

fiords
glacial valleys that have been flooded by the sea

glaciation
climatic conditions where there is a permanent ice cover over an area

Tasman Sea

NEW ZEALAND

Pacific Ocean

South Westland

What can I do?

When I go on walking trips in the natural environment with my mom, we make sure we take all of our trash home with us to get rid of it properly. We're also careful not to pollute streams and rivers with detergents or food scraps.

CASE STUDY — Galapagos Islands, Ecuador

volcanic
an area of Earth's crust where very hot rocks, ashes, and steam break through the surface

iguana
a giant lizard

evolution
the gradual process of change in living things as they adapt to suit their environment

feral
domestic animals that have turned wild and roam the countryside

In the Pacific Ocean, about 620 miles (1,000 km) west of the South American country of Ecuador, there is a group of 19 islands and 40 smaller rock formations and reefs. They were named the Galapagos Islands after the giant tortoises that live there. (*"Galapago"* in the Spanish language means *"saddle."* This refers to the shell of these huge reptiles.) The Galapagos Islands were added to the World Heritage List in 1978.

The area is a very active volcanic region. Three ocean currents also meet there. These two factors, together with the long distance to the South American continent, have created a unique natural environment. Some unusual animals have developed and live in this environment. There are the giant tortoises, the land iguana, and many types of the tiny finch bird.

A scientist, Charles Darwin, studied the unusual life on the Galapagos Islands in 1835. He formed his famous theory of evolution after his stay there.

People have caused some damage to this World Heritage Area:

- Over the past 200 years, more than 100,000 giant tortoises have been killed for their meat and oil.
- Domestic animals such as hogs, donkeys, goats, dogs, and black rats have been taken there. They are now feral and destroy native wildlife.
- The number of settlers and tourists is increasing every year causing garbage problems and damage to nature.

ECUADOR

Galapagos Islands

PERU

Pacific Ocean

Giant's Causeway, Northern Ireland

The Giant's Causeway lies at the foot of the sea cliffs at the tip of Northern Ireland. It is made up of about 40,000 huge black columns poking out of the sea. Scientists have studied these formations over the last 300 years. This has helped them learn more about Earth. The Giant's Causeway was added to the World Heritage List in 1986.

The striking landscape was caused by volcanic activity 50 to 60 million years ago. The huge blocks look like the landscape on the moon. They look so strange that myths have been written about them. The myths tell the story of the giant, Finn McCool, who was a brave soldier and commander of the army of the King of Ireland. He built the blocks to bring his wife to Ireland from across the sea from an island off Scotland.

There are now some private owners along the Giant's Causeway. This worries some people. They think that private owners will not preserve this World Heritage Area in the same way that a government would. Some people want the land returned to the government to look after and preserve for future generations.

myths
imaginary stories about the heroes and gods of a certain place

Valuing the world's heritage

When a cultural or natural site is placed on the World Heritage List, this is not the end of the story. The things that made it worth putting on the list must be preserved. It is not only the responsibility of the international community. It is up to everyone to help value and preserve our world heritage for future generations.

This can only occur if, as global citizens, we take action. Some people think that "action" means protesting or doing something violent. But action can take many forms and can always be peaceful, even in a protest march.

These are some actions that can help us value world heritage:

◎ observing the natural and cultural features in the surroundings
◎ becoming aware of the importance of our common world heritage
◎ telling others that it will become something that cannot be renewed if it is damaged.

Active global citizens can make a difference to valuing the world's heritage. Remember: an idea is only an idea until someone puts it into action.

What can we do?
Global citizens discuss global issues to try to find ways of solving them. There is hope for the planet if global citizens act together.

archaeologists scientists who dig up the remains from people's past lives and study them

archives places where public records and historical documents are kept

carat a measurement of the amount of pure gold in metal

citizen a person who lives in a large group of people who they mix with

conservation keeping areas of the natural environment in their original condition

cultures groups of people with different customs, values, and beliefs

environments natural and built surroundings

evolution the gradual process of change in living things as they adapt to suit their environment

feral domestic animals that have turned wild and roam the countryside

fiords glacial valleys that have been flooded by the sea

generation people of about the same age group and living at the same time

glaciation climatic conditions where there is a permanent ice cover over an area

habitat the place where a plant, animal, or insect lives and reproduces

heritage things from the past and present that are valued and saved for future generations

history the study of past events

iguana a giant lizard

indigenous people groups with the same language and culture who are related to the first people in an area

land rights the right of original peoples to own land, especially sacred tribal grounds

mausoleum a huge burial tomb

military to do with the army

mollusk a soft-bodied sea creature, often having a shell

myths imaginary stories about the heroes and gods of a certain place

national treasures people or things of very special importance to a whole country's history and pride

pharaoh a ruler of ancient Egypt

preserve to keep something safe so that it will last for a long time

restoring repairing something to bring it back to a good condition

runoff the rainwater that runs over the land and into rivers, lakes, and seas

shrines holy places

traditions the parts of a culture that are passed down from generation to generation

uranium a radioactive metal that is used to produce nuclear energy and weapons

urban cities and towns

volcanic an area of Earth's crust where very hot rocks, ashes, and steam break through the surface